Barry Humphries'

A STORY OF LOVE

Barry Humphries'

M

First published 1980 by
THE MACMILLAN COMPANY OF AUSTRALIA PTY LTD
107 Moray Street, South Melbourne 3205
6 George Place, Artarmon 2064

Associated companies in
London and Basingstoke, England
New York Dublin Johannesburg Delhi

National Library of Australia
cataloguing in publication data

Humphries, Barry, 1934–
Barry Humphries' treasury of Australian kitsch.

ISBN 0 333 29955 8

1. Kitsch — Australia. I. title.

709'.94

Set in 10/11 Palatino
Printed at Griffin Press Limited, Marion Road, Netley, South Australia.

Frontispiece: 'Story of Love'.
Fairground award for excellence.

Catalogue

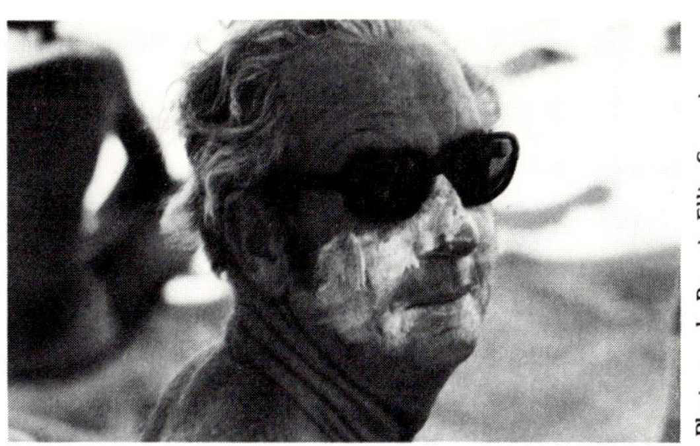

Photograph: Rennie Ellis, Scoopix

Aspects of the Australian Experience.

To the memory of Smacka Fitzgibbon (1930–1979)
Musician
Patriot
and Friend.

I have always suspected public taste to be a mongrel product, out of affectation by dogmatism.

ROBERT LOUIS STEVENSON

Vulgarity is the rich man's modest contribution to democracy.

OSCAR WILDE

La statue sur un palais ou un temple, ainsi qu'au milieu d'un jardin ou d'une place publique, se montre sous différents aspects métaphysiques; au fâite d'un palais, contre le ciel méridional, elle a quelque chose d'homérique, une espèce de joie sévère et lointaine, mêlée de mélancolie. Sur des places publiques son aspect est excessivement surprenant, surtout si son socle est bas, car, dans ce cas, elle paraît se confondre avec l'agitation des hommes et la vie quotidienne de la ville.

GIORGIO DE CHIRICO

All creative art must rise out of a specific soil, and flicker with a sense of place.

D. H. LAWRENCE

Photograph: Peter Thomson, Melbourne

The Author

Introduction

It is a wonder and a joy to the author of this volume to think that it will be translated into some thirty-seven languages, and that its simultaneous publication in Western Europe, the Americas and the South-East Asian continent from which it draws its inspiration will place it within the reach of two thirds of the world's literate population.

No single art book, let alone one which surveys the total panorama of the Australian aesthetic achievement, has addressed itself to so immense a public.

It is, however, a sobering thought that some millions of these readers will be encountering the word 'Australia' for the first time; whilst others who have hitherto believed themselves to be authorities on all forms of Oceanian culture will be forced to abandon their previously held theories and start afresh. For here, in this compendium of images, is the first cultural encephalograph of the Australoid Race*.

At last the constraints and distortions of a degenerate European methodology have been purged and the subversive legacy of mandarin myopics like Berenson, Burckhardt, Wölfflin and Panofsky have been utterly eliminated.

For too long now we have silently suffered the slights and calumnies of the *Ausländer* and in the cultural chronographies of cosmopolitan critics one may search in vain for so much as an exiguous footnote on Australian art.

But a new dawn has broken, and in its clear light can be seen the marmoreal outline of a unique and virile Australian *Weltanschauung*.

Yet, although this is essentially an art book and a work of original scholarship, the reader will be disappointed if he seeks herein the specious jargon of the aesthetician or the arid taxonomy of a text book, for this is above all a work addressed to simple people. To Australian people.

The images which follow are an inventory of their birthright. They are strong images. Powerful images. Present them in any order and their message will be the same. Elements apparently disparate speak with a single voice: the man-made aluminium bottle opener in the form of the Sydney Opera House springs as naturally from the mainstream of Australian art as do the dancing *débutantes* at the Sulphide Welfare Club, Newcastle. Similarly the exposed aggregate urinal and the deadly Slipper Spider are, so to speak, a single chord upon different instruments, the Skyline-of-Melbourne hearth-rug and the Jenolan Caves but twin avatars of the same divinity.

I have found it helpful, particularly to the students who accompany me on my walking tours, to elucidate this notion by reference to the Platypus, a creature which has been so plausibly confected from fin, fur and feather as to imply the intrusion of some supra-historical *artistic* intelligence at the blueprint stage.

The reader, of whatever race, colour or bias, cannot but be struck by the uncanny homogeneity of the artefacts as they unfold within the pages of this volume. One might even be persuaded that some Jungian synergic principle underlies them all. The present writer finds himself unable to avoid the conclusion that a *genetic* link between man-made and natural forms in Australia is nothing if not inescapable.

If this conclusion should appear far-fetched I invite the reader to confirm it by means of the following simple test. Let him subject that priceless and masterly geological formation known as 'The Three Sisters' (q.v.) to a topological laser scan (taking each sister singly). Let him display the resulting hologram in digital form and compare it with a braille transcript of 'The Don Lane Show' as seen on Channel Nine. If he should then be prepared to dismiss the point-for-point identity of the two print-outs as 'mere coincidence', I beg leave to doubt his sanity and to sanction the curtailment of his propagative powers.

There is no doubt in my mind that the publication of this book and the dissemination of its message will precipitate a vast cavalcade of the curious: artists, naturalists, teratologists, and scholars — such a motley as invaded Easter Island when its high-camp megaliths were first promoted.

So tantalizing and irresistibly seductive is the glimpse of Australia this book affords that we must expect the envious foreigner and his brethren to overwhelm our harbours and our aerodromes in their hundreds, and then in their hundreds of thousands. I defy the most *blasé* of my readers, or the most incorrigibly sessile, to glance at the pictorial matter within these covers and not feel impelled to feast his eyes and gorge his senses on the objects themselves.

For too long our remote sub-continent has attracted a type of tourist interested in little other than the surf, the sun, and the turf. But in extending our hospitality, as soon we shall, to a multitude of clamouring art lovers we could expose ourselves to a new peril. Australians know only too well that

---

* Soon to be released as a major motion picture.

the trans-hemispheric art world is rife with prancing catamites and predatory mamelukes who would dearly love to introduce their Chaldean practices to Australia's blameless shores.

It is common knowledge that ours is the only country in the world which has freed itself of unnatural vice by requiring a blood test of each visa applicant.

But I digress.

It now gives me immeasurable satisfaction, not untinged with old-fashioned patriotic pride, to be your guide and psychopomp on the journey that lies ahead of us. Together we will marvel at the malls of Melbourne — the Florence of Australian cities — with its celebrated 'Cincinnatti end' of Collins Street. Here, in park, boulevard and plaza, swept by the ceaseless winds for which the city is famous, admire with me the ubiquitous citrus tints which alike drench tram-car, phone kiosk and car rental hostess. In Sydney's Martin Place let us clamber together through its burgeoning forest of multi-hued amenities or witness a Rotarian dinner or stock car race on the stage of the conch-roofed Opera House, Casino and multi-purpose Conference, Function and Convention Complex. Then on to the fountains of Brisbane which, like so many in Australia, employ water with such delightful reticence, and to the abstract sculptures which invest Perth with a ferruginous grandeur that only iron oxide can impart.

I have not mentioned the gaudy aboriginal opals or the parrot-hued easel paintings which enrich the visual life of Australia's most humble inhabitant. Neither have I dwelt on the remarkable properties of the antipodean climate which has the extraordinary power to preserve and embalm *style*, so that, for example, the mini-skirt mode of fifteen years ago imperishably survives to chafe the mottled loins of pert shopgirl and grizzled bus conductress. Herein, peradventure, lies some promise of permanence for the noblest of our artefacts — proof against that transience which attends all of man's finest creations.

Till now I have but proffered titillating appetizers to the Last Lucullan Supper of antipodean Taste which awaits you all.

And be assured that the dishes which ballast this banquet in such graveolent profusion are so ambrosian in their nature that you may gorge yourselves in total freedom without fear either of gustatory discomfort or, indeed, of satiety.

Go forth and enjoy yourselves. *Mahlzeit!*

Heidelberg, August 1980

Meyer D Altson 1881–1965
Winged Words (Portrait of the Artist's Wife). 1926
Oil on canvas, 49¼" x 35¼"
Bequeathed by M D Altson, 1967

Reproduced by permission of the National Gallery of Victoria, Melbourne

Time and space do not permit me to mine more than a few gems from the rich seam that is Antipodean Art. In fact, I have found it more difficult to decide what to *omit* from these pages than to decide which examples to include.

CLIFTON PUGH

'Leda and the Emu'

26 September — 13 October 1979

CRANE KALMAN GALLERY

▲ The invitation to view a celebrated artist's *Kunstzyklus* in which myth and marsupial go, so to speak, hand in wing (*viz.* 'Europa and the Wombat').

Austral Arcadia. 'The Music Lesson' (1904) by Sydney Long (1871–1955).

Rural Social Realism. 'Sunday Evening' (1940) by Sir Russell Drysdale (1912-   ).

Magpie tram by Clifton Pugh.

Photograph: Rennie Ellis, Scoopix

Great artists as great artists see them. The Poetess Dame Mary Gilmore painted in 1957 by Sir William Dobell (1899–1970) and the Melbourne-based Actress and *Diseuse* Dame Edna Everage executed in 1969 by John Brack (1920–).

The Face of Australia here captured by the brush of Albert Tucker.

Utilitarian Art. This beautiful textile, hand-painted with evocative native scenes, is here displayed on the most successful piece of mobile sculpture ever wrought by an Australian hand – Hills's 'Rotary Clothes Hoist' (*circa* ?).

Art for export. Famous and original works by Australian-based artists are here caringly crated for shipment to *connoisseurs* in every corner of the globe. Note realistic pricing structure in the A.D.R. (Australian Democratic Republic).

Privilege Offer

Pearce and Hughes announce the release of a limited edition of their Silver Yabby Pendant.

This finely detailed representation of Australia's famous freshwater crustacean is cast in solid sterling silver, and with its delicate silver chain weighs fully seven grams.

Only one thousand of these pendants will be struck — order now to avoid disappointment.

Your Silver Yabby is presented in an elegant kid leat er pouch.

ONLY

$29.00

To Pearce & Hughes
Please send me   Silver Yabby Pendants.

Please allow at least three weeks for your order to be processed. A receipt will be issued directly your money is received.

Name

Address

Post Code

Pearce & Hughes, 103 Purnell Rd., Corio, Geelong, 3214.

This etched depiction of Sydney's Bohemian life in the 1920s is not merely an accurate piece of social realism: its iconography is as apposite for the 80s as it ever was when the internationally acclaimed Australian-based artist, Norman Lindsay (1879–1969), first took out his burin and laid it on the copper.

Operatic millinery. The famous Australian-based Actress and Mega-Star, Dame Edna Everage D.B.E., modelled this creation at the 1976 Royal Ascot Races. It was inspired, of course, by the internationally acclaimed Sydney Opera House, Casino and multi-purpose Conference, Function and Convention Complex (q.v.).

Disappearing Sydney. This striking mosaic relief on a Rushcutters Bay *façade* was completely obliterated in 1979, and if restoration were undertaken — as well it may be after publication of this volume — it could cost the rate-payer dearly.

Thrifty Melbournians whose memories go back to the austere 1950s will recollect the day this gay, futuristic, ceramic mural enlivened their ingress to a city banking hall, thus setting a stylistic fashion many were to follow.

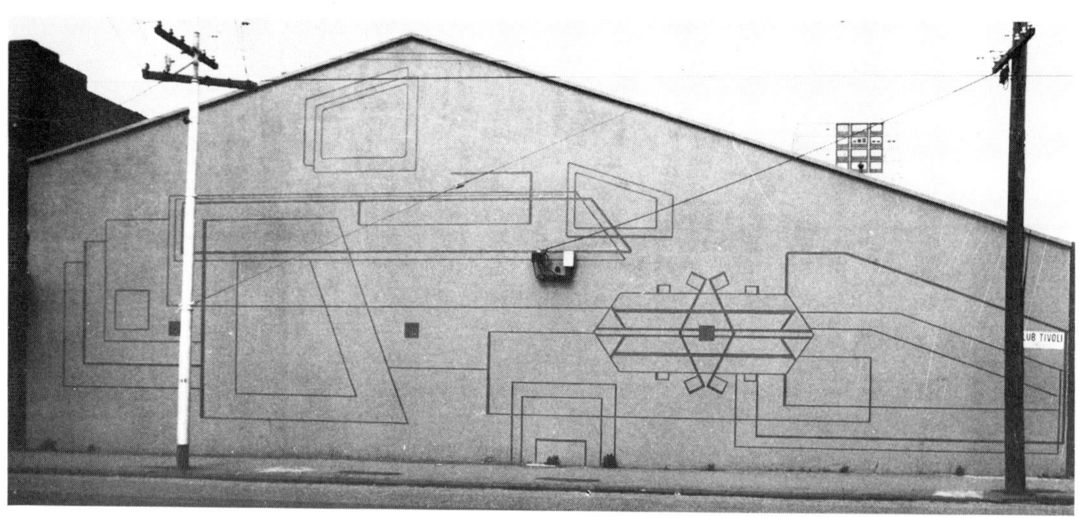

Undistinguished Melbourne walls transformed by the cunning hand of the abstract artist.

This typical exterior mural in an industrial suburb movingly unfolds the diurnal saga of Austral toil.

31 ST. MARTINS TOWER

EIIR
OUR ARBOUR

Above left: What vestibule fresco more vividly illustrates the rapturous awakening of an Australian visual consciousness in the seventh decade of the twentieth century? Note twin influences of Miró and Abo.

Left: Fences and *façades*. The world will never forget — so long as this magnificent mosaic mural survives — the triumphant 1956 Ballarat Olympiad.

Brass name-plate for an Australian suburban villa, *circa* 1910, featuring popular local fauna — in this case two jovial Australian kookaburra birds (q.v.) with a reptile-framed name panel descending from their beaks. Artist untraceable as this book went to press.

Beau Brummel Australian-style: the everyday habiliments of a Southern Hemispheric He-man. Most thinking Australian men prefer to don apparel which celebrates some zoological, technological and topographical aspect of their unique environment.

Newly arrived Eastern Mediterraneans have applied themselves, and their age-old skills, with gusto to the creation and the embellishment of soft furnishings. Demand for these educational upholstered visual aids in hand-painted velvet has soared, to the extent that many now bear a Japanese *griffe*.

Few discerning Australians would evacuate their dottle into any receptacle other than a ceramic gum-leaf, or accept cream if not proffered from the beak or muzzle of a beloved marsupial.

Meat and confectionery (q.v.) are two Australian staples which benefit from their purveyors' sound command of the aesthetics of merchandising. Note the traditional 'mini' adopted by this staid Sydney *vendeuse*.

Stylish monumental *bas relief* on the upper *façade* of the Fletcher Jones trouser show-rooms, Flinders Street, Melbourne, Victoria. *Circa* 1940. Height: 8′ 6″. Made by Picton Hopkins Australia Pty Ltd to a design based on artwork produced by an unknown English commercial artist.

Vegetables in the service of Art. Prizewinners in the Interpretative and Free Expression Division of the Floral Arts Society of Victoria, 1978: driftwood and succulent unite in an unequivocal statement.

Photograph: Nucolorvue Productions Pty Ltd

Kangaroo paw or *Anigozanthos manglesii*. Marsupial foot-fetishists with an horticultural bias are keen cultivators of this curious bloom which rivals the Gladiolus as Australia's national flower.

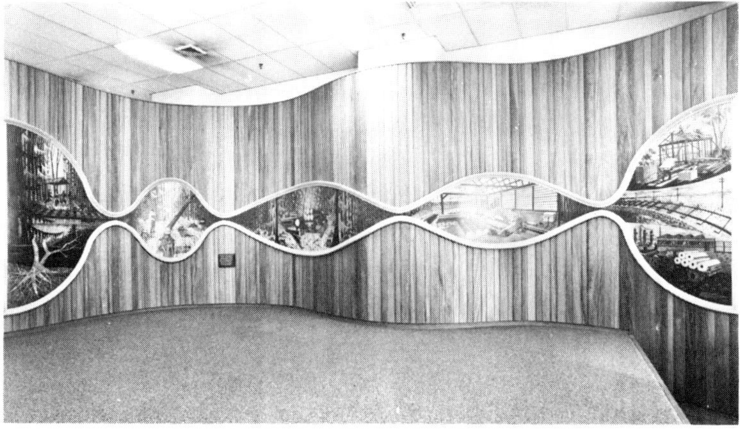

This inlaid wood mural was designed and executed by Leslie Senty for the Forestry Commission of N.S.W.

Depicting various phases of forestry and the timber industry, the mural is made from many thousands of pieces of wood veneer each individually cut to shape to form the finished work.

The Mural was unveiled by
The Hon. Wal. Fife, M.L.A.
Minister for Conservation.
23rd FEBRUARY 1972

A marvellous message in marquetry: a mighty forest died that Art might live.

HYDE PARK
SQUARE

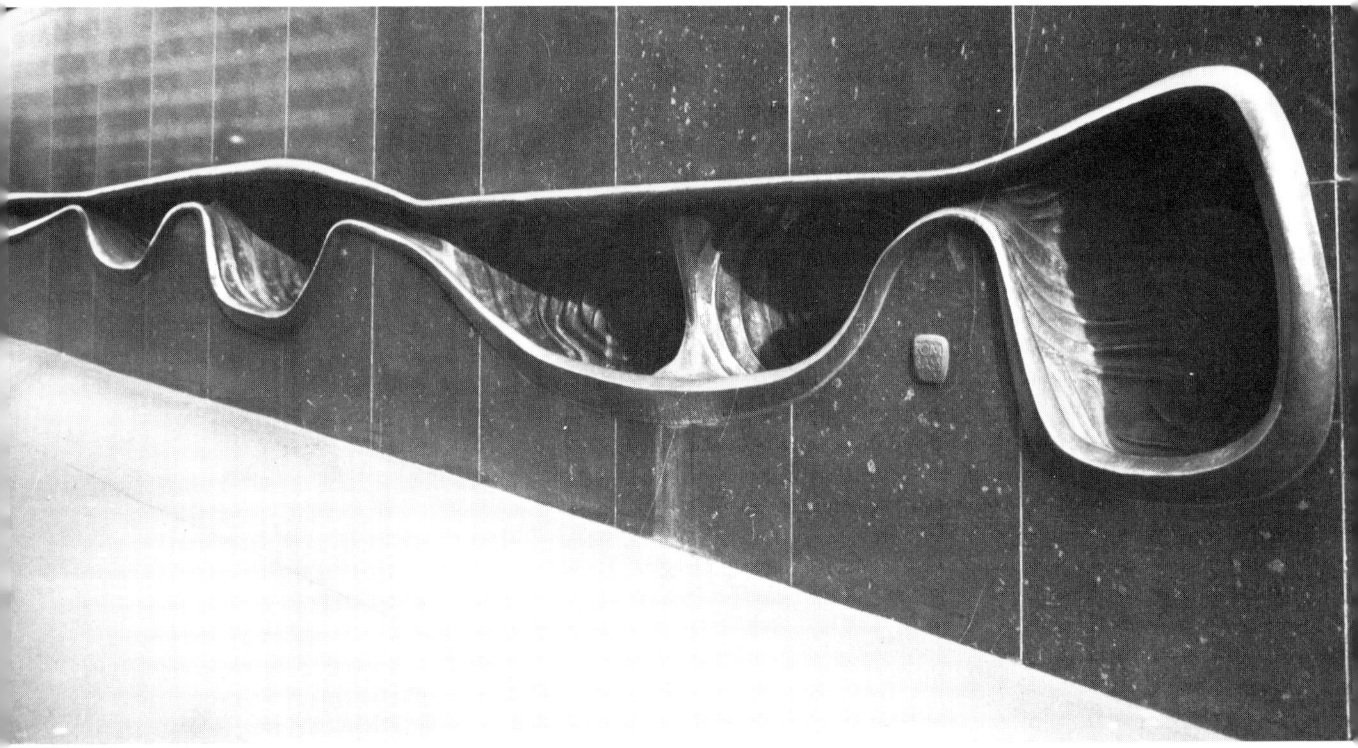

Left: Wonderful ways with water. Reticence and aquatic conservation are the keynotes of these Sydney-based fountains.

Below left: The allure this functional free-form fountain holds for Sydney's nocturnal fontaphiles has necessitated round-the-clock surveillance by the New South Wales hard-pressed water police.

The 'Black Stump' fountain in Chifley Square (*circa* 1969), permanently dehydrated, thrusting defiantly skyward through dwarfed verdure.

Water conservation is once again the keynote of this Sydney fountain design (*circa* 1966) at the Colonial Sugar Refinery building. Note reptile skin finish.

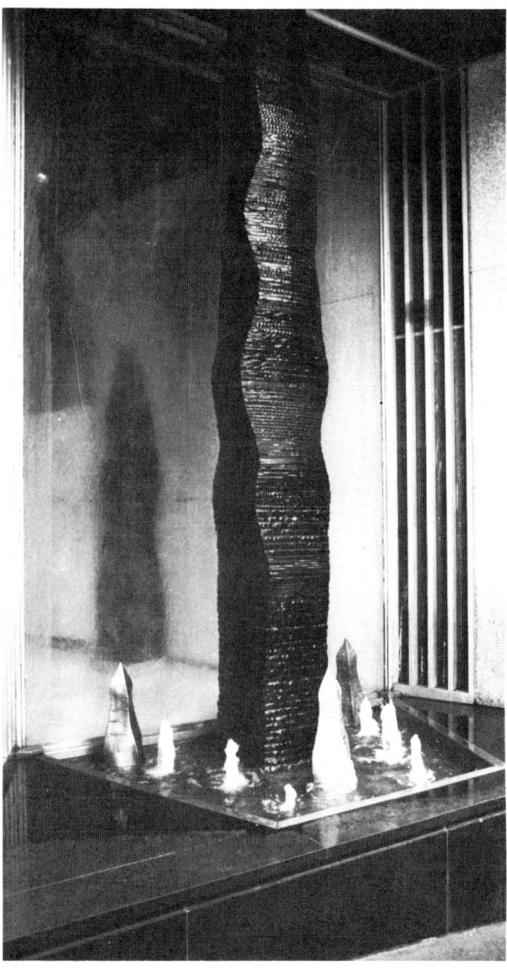

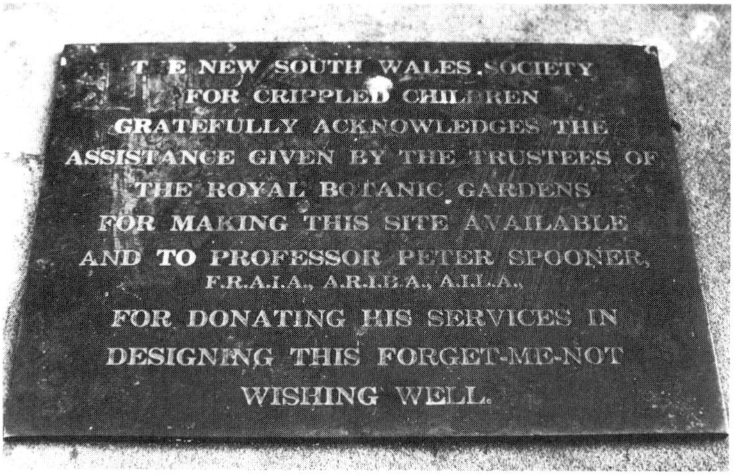

The popular expectorating toad fountain and wishing well in Macquarie Street, Sydney. Another beloved Australian reptile is here commemorated.

OLGA LODGE FOUNTAIN

THIS FOUNTAIN FORMS THE CENTREPIECE
OF THE SOUTHERN PLAZA ENVIRONMENTAL
SCULPTURE DESIGNED BY O. H. HAJEK, WHICH
WAS DECLARED OPEN BY HER MAJESTY
THE QUEEN ON 22ND MARCH, 1977.

A Perth *Treffpunkt*. This brace of colossal decapitated metal emus (q.v.) strides insouciantly along its rusticated plinth of *bonsai* bush-land at the cosmopolitan corner of St George's Terrace and the Parmelia Freeway.

Oblivious to the work of his Perth *confrère*, yet seized by the same *Zeitgeist*, a Brisbane landscape architect has created an ensemble of truncated forms which half remind one of Australia's indigenous race.

A range of popular garden ornaments.
Marsupial optional.

Few multi-storey car-parks in the world can boast a more opulent plaza fountain than this prestigious Commonwealth precinct with its multi-hued *assemblage* and attentive staff of fountaineers.

The tank-traps of Vietnamese confrontation are evoked in these thrusting virile forms, symbolizing the Adelaide Festival of the Arts. No expense has been spared in this gay orchestration of form and reinforced concrete — a colourful example of Australian plaza-planning (*viz.* p. 92 — open space as obstacle race).

The lucullan nature of the proletarian breakfast is always a talking point amongst visiting trade union delegations to the A.D.R. (Australian Democratic Republic).
This routine surveillance photograph from a strategically placed miniaturized guest scanner shows a typical range of down-under dawn refreshments available to the overseas visitor. Note drowsy pineapple segments.

A typical Queensland home.

Right: Bottle as Belvedere.
Recycling Australian style.

Below: Mollusc as Motel
The influence of modern European architecture, translated into the quaint local Australian vernacular, is everywhere evident. In this arresting sea-side hotel, conference and convention centre near Adelaide, however, the mannerisms of le Courbusier and Mies van der Rohe are not at once discernible.

The 'Rose Fountain', Roselands Shopping Centre (*circa* 1965; height: 16 ft) with its fifteen hand-beaten copper petals and 135 'thorn' spouts. This Sydney show-piece has often been criticized for its excessive use of ratepayers' water.

A FOUNTAIN OF MEANING

A 3.5-metre high symbolic fountain will be erected by the Chamber of Mines in front of the central railway station in Wellington Street.

A model of the fountain is on display in the National Bank in St George's Terrace.

The $70,000 fountain is the mining industry's gift to the State for its 150th anniversary.

The fountain will symbolise earth, fire and ater and man's related challenge to the elements for his advancement.

It will be built of a diorite, at the eastern end of a reflective pool, with river-washed stones complementing the diorite pyramid, symbolising earth.

A big stainless steel plane, which will reflect the sun's rays throughout the day, will symbolise fire.

Within the split pyramid, stainless steel conduits and atomising nozzles will produce a cloud effect.

The entire sculpture will be reflected in a pool.

The sculptor, chosen after a number of local artists had submitted designs, is Mr Frank Wilkinson (33).

Mr Wilkinson is a lecturer in scuplture and three dimensional design at the Perth Technical College.

The *West Australian*, Wednesday 18 July 1979. 'Miss Lorraine Nayler, of Hamersley, with a model of the fountain'.

Awards for Australian-based Artistic Excellence

These coveted and striking statuettes in metal and perspex are also a boon to Australian-based sculptors, offering them a welcome chance to liberate themselves from the influences of Henry Moore, Barbara Hepworth and Lyn Chadwick.

Collection: John Meillon

Collection: Magnus Nankervis & Curl

Collection: Margaret Fink

Collection: John Meillon

Collection: Bill Harding

Collection: John Meillon

Australian history has found its finest expression in enduring works of sculpture. Here, two generations ponder what this virile figure — in Sydney's shady park-side Macquarie Street — is about to unfold for their edification.

In contrast to the restrained eroticism of the sculpture reproduced opposite, the creator of this impudent monolith leaves little to the imagination. It is an organic coral carving with its own sensuous pool of reflection, and forms a popular *Treffpunkt* for art-loving Melbournians on rare windless days.

PLEASE
DO NOT
TOUCH
ARTWORK

The Authorities are introducing stern measures to discourage the incorrigibly tactile art-loving Australian from caressing commissioned monuments such as Ian Mackay's 'Funnel' (installed June 1978; of austenitic steel; height: 16 ft). Local bird-life (q.v.) unfortunately does not fall within the Authorities' jurisdiction and this work is already a firm favourite with 'our feathered friends'.

Four of Australia's legendary folk characters, Dad and Dave, Mum and Mabel, are soon to be added to Gundagai's list of tourist attractions. Larger than life size copper statues of the famous quartette are to be erected at the Tout Family's Snake Gully tourist complex, five miles north of Gundagai opposite the Dog on the Tucker Box pioneers memorial.

Australia's best loved monument and adjacent amenities are to be encountered five miles outside the New South Wales town of Gundagai. This petrified canine, atop his master's viands and victuals, testifies to the dumb devotion of the Australian dingo, and inspires in the breasts of Australians the same *Weltschmerzstimmungsgefühl* as the Brandenburger Tor does in ours.

Australian heroes (an occasional series)

The cement polygon seeming to salute a telegraph pole in this plate is a larger-than-life representation of Captain James Cook, noted syphilitic and discoverer of Australia, whose tropical landfall occurred in close proximity to this eponymous motor hotel.

Right: **Public lavatory as Rural homestead**. In this forward-thinking hospitably verandahed ranch-style building, harmoniously sited in Sydney's harbour-side parkland, the unknown municipal architect has incorporated several arresting features , including a possum- and vandal-proof solar energy trap and a *third* door for the convenience of a category of Australian visitor as yet undetermined.

Below: **Bank as Cromlech**. Megalithic Melbourne is justly proud of this exuberant addition to its internationally acclaimed skyline. Many a metropolis might wish that it had at least *one* structure of this calibre, but for Melbournians — denizens of the world's thirty-eighth largest city — such a sculptural agglomeration of brickwork is commonplace!

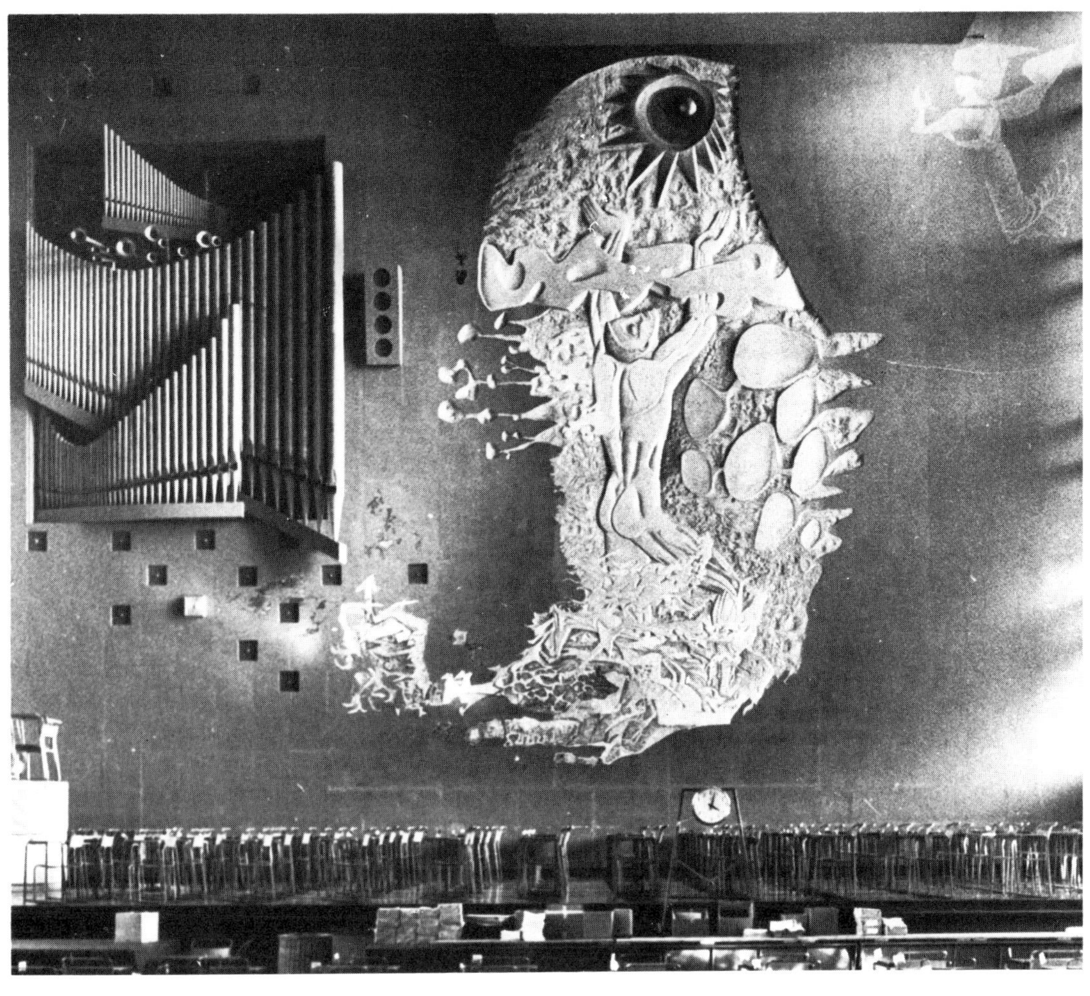

A generation of Melbourne's top professional men and women sat their final examinations in the shadow of this inspirational work (*circa* 1956) in which their own aspirations and academic struggles, in an Australian context, are symbolized and sublimated.

The eponymous dedicatee of this popular pool was a former Australian Prime Minister who allegedly perished in a swimming accident.

The Great Barrier Coral Reef, pinned like a piece of intricate polyp-wrought costume jewellery to the broad bosom of north-east Australia. Here proud Queenslanders admire this popular growth through a transparent bottom.

Conservation Australian-style. Perth's sprawling nineteenth-century barracks were demolished to make way for this international-style motorway. However, a tiny band of committed conservationists won a rare victory and the historic portal (arrowed) has been preserved on a traffic island, where its fairy-tale fabric subtly complements the thrusting skyline that is the Western Australian capital.

The *animalier's* art. Australasian sculpture has always kept a low profile (q.v.) and this undeservedly overlooked example is no exception. This mosaic tortoise (Length: 10′ 6″; width: 6′ 6″; height: 1′ 6″. Material: concrete, faced with slate. Designed and installed 1966) reclines in the gardens of the Fletcher Jones Trouser Factory, Warrnambool, Victoria. Australian-based reptile sculptors have indeed found a generous and discerning patron in this famous tailoring firm.

The wrought ironsmiths of Australia are the envy of other nations and this comparatively restrained example draws its inspiration from the Commonwealth's nocturnal insect life, in the shape of a life-size representation of the harmless Melbourne Marmite moth.

Australia's breakfast companion: the ubiquitous koala-up-a-gum-tree catsup dispenser, in realistic hand-crafted biscuit-ware.

A striking, and not un-typical up-state diner and its grassy plaza, in a land of many delightful surprises. The building itself is imaginatively constructed along the lines of an Australian cow.

Marsupial missive, or roo-skin postcard. Note apposite philatelic exhortation on *verso*.

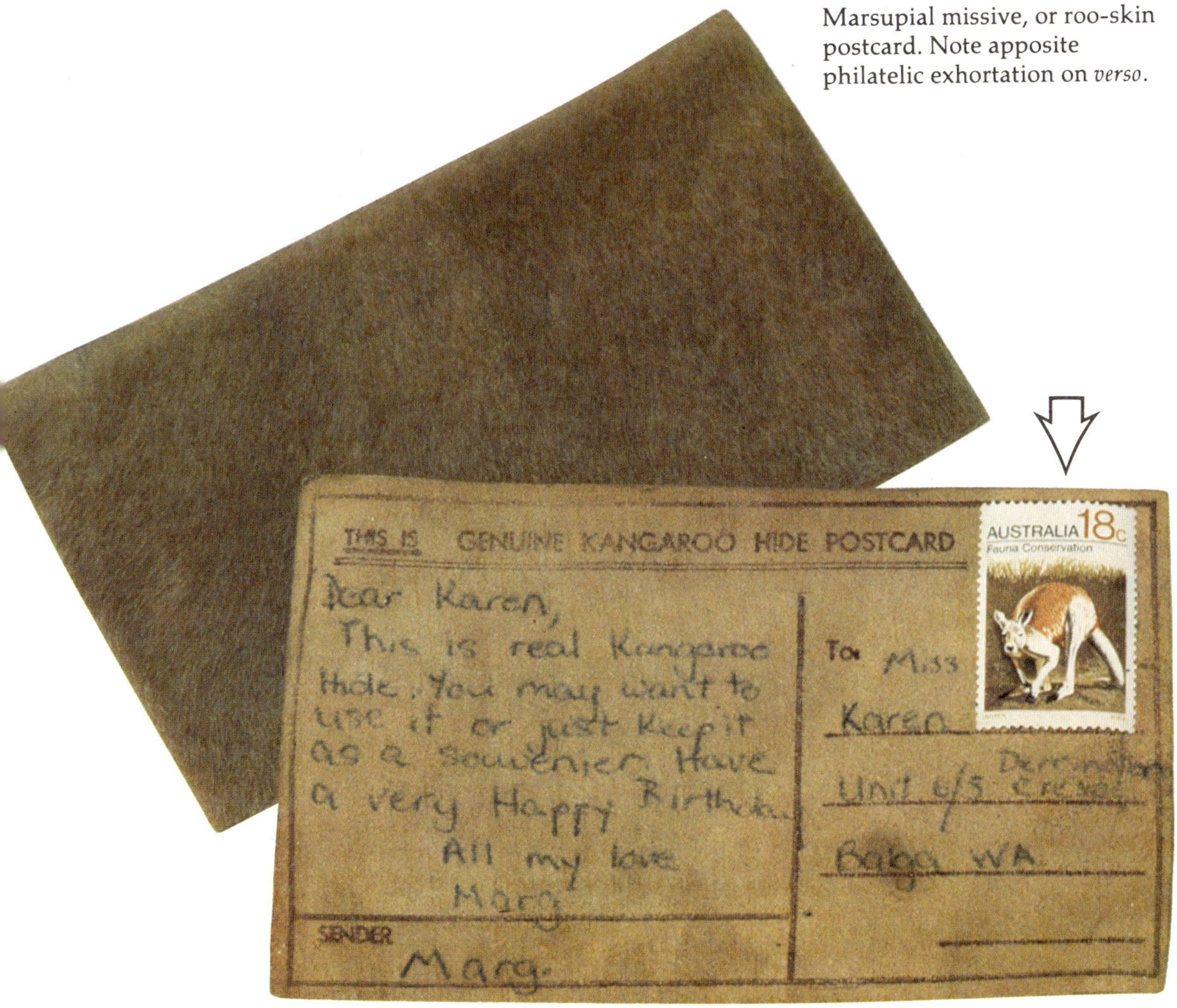

THIS IS GENUINE KANGAROO HIDE POSTCARD

AUSTRALIA 18c
Fauna Conservation

Dear Karen,
This is real Kangaroo hide. You may want to use it or just keep it as a souvenier. Have a very Happy Birthday
All my love
Marg

SENDER
Marg

To Miss
Karen
Unit 6/5 Derrington Cresc.
Balga WA

Utilitarian Art
Australian-style.

Photograph: Rennie Ellis, Scoopix

In the fifth decade of the twentieth century Australian design took its Great Leap Forward. Here, juxtaposed, are two milestones in antipodean styling – the Australian-based 'Holden' saloon (*foreground*) and the Sydney Opera House, Casino and multi-purpose Conference, Function and Convention Complex (*rear*) (q.v.). Note striking stylistic affinities.

Ethnic minorities are often given permission by the Municipal Police Authorities, under certain exceptional circumstances, to construct and put into practice their age-old energy-conserving devices, evinced here by this not untypical residence in 'Little Holland', South Australia.

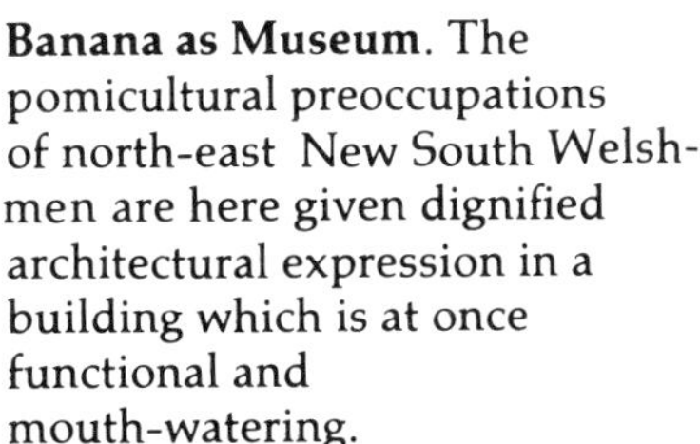

Banana as Museum. The pomicultural preoccupations of north-east New South Welshmen are here given dignified architectural expression in a building which is at once functional and mouth-watering.

Photograph: Nambucca Guardian News

Theatre Australia. Always relevant, this scene from an internationally acclaimed award-winning Australian production casts a concerned Brechtian glance at recent events in Iran.

Visitors to Australia are always impressed by its cosmopolitan cuisine, and particularly by the east Mediterranean specialities which youthful Australoids are finding more and more to their taste. A combination of nutritious diet, sunshine and genetic stability has evolved a race of young men and women whose sophistication and wholesome sexuality are the envy of lands outside the A.D.R.

The 'National' Gallery of Victoria and adjacent amenities.

Photographs: Rennie Ellis, Scoopix

AMP AMP
MLC
PARMELIA HILTON
ROYAL
PORTUGAL
ITALY
SALVADOR
CHILE
COSTA RICA
SRI LANKA
GUATEMALA

The Western Australian-based city of Perth was unanimously selected as the *venue* for the winter 1979 Miss Universe adjudication. The vying international lovelies (*foreground*) seem to be lapping up their first bush-land experience.

Australia has just discovered what beauty lies within her bowels. Here, tired office personnel relax and re-charge their batteries in subterranean Sydney. Boy meets girl; stalactite meets stalagmite.

Tourists from all over the world flock to the Blue Mountains, New South Wales – Sydney's Mount Rushmore – in order to marvel at the famous 'Three Sisters'.
Due to the unblinking munificence of the Australian Council for the Arts, this majestic escarpment of living rock is being transformed by award-winning Australian-based sculptpersons into a frieze of uncannily life-like *colossi*. The 'Three Sisters' *already* completed (pictured, left to right) represent a trio of Australia's more rugged pioneers of feminism – Ms Eliza Fraser, Dame Nellie Melba and Doctor Germaine Greer. 'In the pipeline' are Ms Olivia Newton-John, O.B.E., Ms Barbara Blackman and Ms Margaret Fink.

Photographs : Rennie Ellis, Scoopix

The detritus of innocent Austral pleasure. Any sporting venue in the A.D.R. at 6 pm on a Saturday, and an example of 'macho' millinery favoured by the fashion-conscious Australoid athlete.

This exquisitely tended knoll with its complement of trim native shrubbery tastefully terminating Melbourne's principal artery, The St Kilda Road, exemplifies the single-minded aesthetic preoccupations of Australian-based urban planners.

Ornamental terracotta accretion suggestive of the form of Australia's preferred marsupial, and a welcome variation on the ubiquitous wyverns and gryphons which decorate the gables of Melbourne's Queen Anne homes (*circa* 1910).

A corner of a typical Australian formal garden. Note striking resemblance between the three trees and the upper torso of the *Bettongia cuniculus* or Tasmanian Rat-Kangaroo (seen in profile). The opportunity must here be seized to correct the widespread, albeit erroneous, belief that these Australian trees *naturally* conform to the contours of the popular marsupial. The phenomenon is invariably the work of the Tasmanian topiarist.

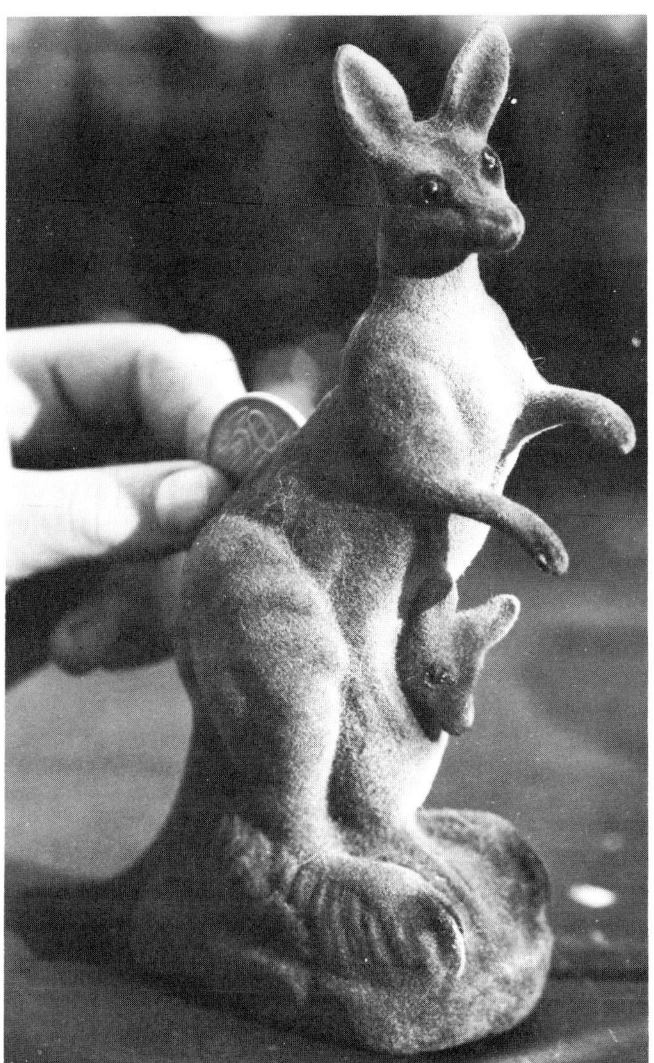

Marsupial as money box. In the antipodes it is not generally known that the kangaroo is emblematic of thrift and far-sightedness. Nor is it generally known that the exhortation 'look before you leap' derives from an aboriginal pictograph.
Height: $9\frac{3}{4}''$
Material: Fibrous plastic
Made in Hong Kong

Detail: obverse

Photograph: Newcastle Morning Herald

The *corps de ballet* at the Sulphide Welfare Club, Newcastle. They are left to right: Gay McNaughton, Joan Collins, Lola Anderson, Jean Forde and Thea Johanson.
Marching — whilst not yet compulsory in freedom-loving Australia — is warmly encouraged by State leaders (with the exception, perhaps, of Queensland). Apparel the average Australian in a spruce uniform, strike up the martial music, and a predominantly gay spectacle will unfold, whatever the age or sex of the participants.

North Cronulla life-saving club leading a recent parade.

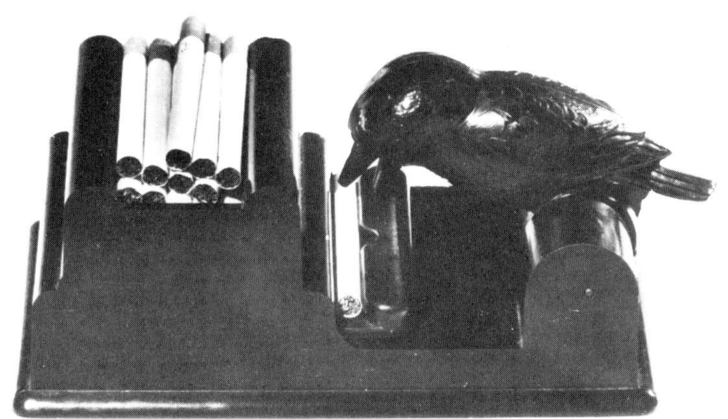

The smoking jackass. Nothing is too much trouble for Australian birdlife, whose quality of helpfulness is vividly portrayed in this Bakelite cigarette ejector and popular smoker's aid (ideally teamed with a bronzed koala ashtray). The beloved kangaroos have also lent a hand in furnishing every Australian home with the nation's most popular bar-tool.

Photograph: Rennie Ellis, Scoopix

Inspired by the profile of his native island continent, this itinerant Alice Springs *rocailliste* poses proudly at one of his recent retrospectives.

What the sacred Mount Fuji was to Utamaro and Hokusai, the skylines of Sydney and Melbourne have long been to the weavers and *tapissiers* of the south-east.

MELBOURNE SKYLINE

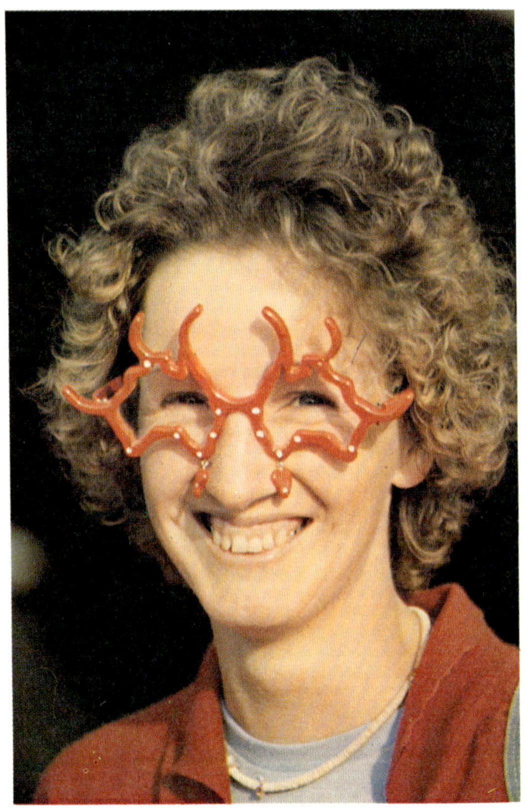

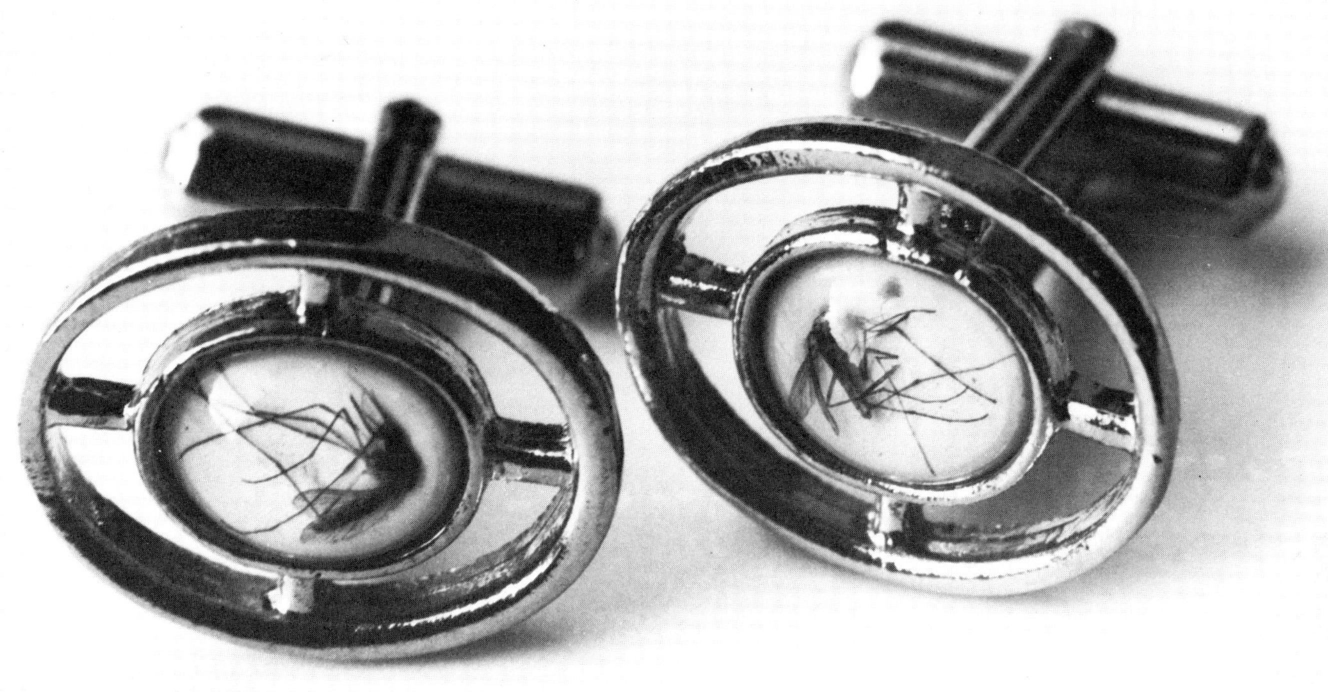

Of all racial types, the Australian is the most insatiably visual — a fact which it is perhaps unnecessary to point out to students of this volume. The Australian is forever on the *'qui vive'* lest any element in his teeming environment elude his all-encompassing purview. This essentially *vigilant* quality is very remarkably expressed in the tools he has evolved to aid him in the apprehension of his own peculiar *Lebenserfahrung* and his striving to understand and come to terms with *la condition australienne*.

Left: A range of typically elaborate and exceedingly beautiful eyewear is modelled here by a group of persons photographed at random outside a Kalgoorlie conference centre and casino complex.

Australian malarial mosquitoes make a striking and attractive pair of cuff-links (seen here actual size) — a boon to the wrist-conscious Australian male. Affectionately referred to by their diminutive ('mozzies') these delightful creatures are exclusively bred on Bribie Island, north of Brisbane, for Queensland's thriving State-owned cuff-link conglomerate. The hand-selected 'mozzies' are humanely terminated and entombed in capsules of best quality, sterilized (patent-pending) Austrolex, which are next mounted in handsome hand-crafted seven carat gold settings. Blow-flies ('blowies') are also hand-raised for high-fashion accessories.

Minted marsupials — 'pocket money' — Australia's twenty cent platypus coin (*left*) and one cent possum piece.

KANGAROO PELTS AND RUGS

After careful and selective culling of Kangaroos in far North Queensland plague areas, we have selected choice Kangaroo fur and hides to be made into beautiful rugs, handbags, purses, wallets and Koala Bears.
These soft lovely furs have to be seen to be believed.
Ideal gifts to take home.

BOOMERANGS

We have large stocks of genuine returning Aboriginal made boomerangs, also artifacts and bark paintings. We are tucked away in the low rent area in the Queen Victoria Market building — a tram ride will get you the best prices in town.
Bullock hides, sheepskins etc.

Souvenirs and Gifts

AUSTRALIAN SOUVENIRS

koalas, boomerangs
kangaroo skins, hand bags
purses, teaspoons
bracelets, wallets, key cases
opals, playing cards
ashtrays, scarves, dolls
tea towels, hanks; charms

Fauna – Federal and Fiscal. The escutcheon of Nationhood and its supporters – a rodent saltatory (*left*) and a cassowary erect (*right*) – here dominating the imposing exposed aggregate (q.v.) *façade* of the new and indestructible Federal Court of Australia in Sydney and the estates of the humble.

The sensuous nature of the Australian renders him peculiarly susceptible to texture, and the pragmatic and aesthetic qualities of **exposed aggregate** have proven a boon to Austral architects and 'the man in the street' — as my picture amply illustrates. The Authorities are planning ultimately to re-surface *every* building in the land with this masculine yet sensitive cladding, a 'look' which is, strange to say, already imposing itself on the national diet . Patrons using such a facility must, of course, be prepared to 'take the rough with the smooth'.

Australia's presence at Expo '70 at Osaka, Japan, was movingly expressed by this six million dollar pavilion of sport, culture and scientific achievement — the 'Skyhook'.

Overleaf: Merino mules. These universally worn flocculent foot-warmers are not solely favoured by the Australian housewife *en déshabillée*. The invitingly dark and humid interiors of these popular 'environments for the feet' are a favoured nesting place for the fecund funnel-web, or deadly slipper spider. My plate depicts a dawn encounter familiar to many recently roused Australians.

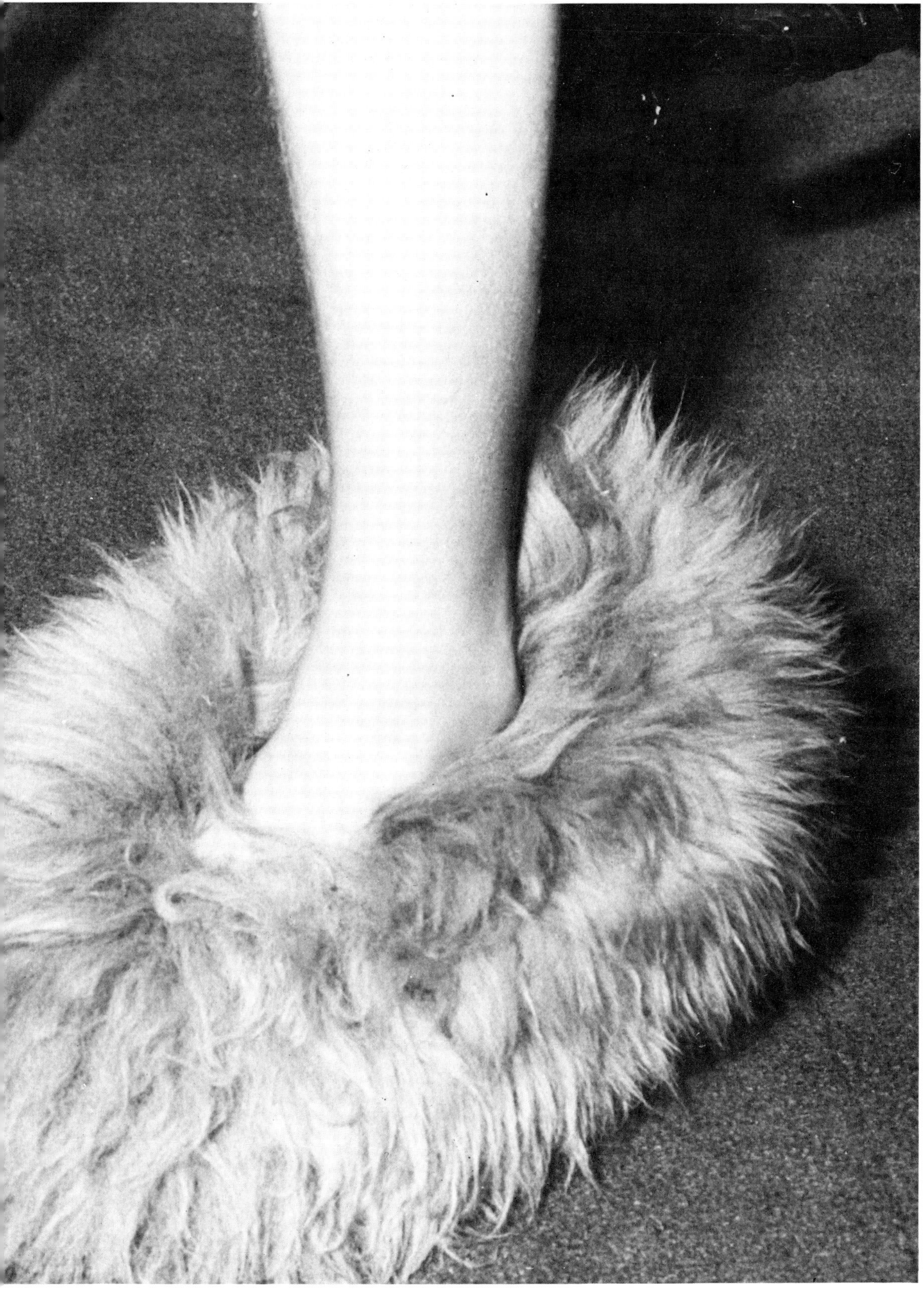

These decorative and *echt*-Australian objects are emblematic of the nation's three *most* popular recreations – drinking, smoking and listening to works from the operatic *repertoire* – sometimes simultaneously. On this page, and opposite, the edifice depicted is, in all instances, the Sydney-based Opera House, Casino and multi-purpose Conference, Function and Convention Complex (q.v.) which is, even now, making Melbournians look to their laurels.

OPERA HOUSE

Fruit as style-setter. Tourists may puzzle as to why New York is known as 'The Big Apple' but they are not slow to realize how Melbourne earned its now-standard universal pomicultural appellation: 'The Big Orange'. The benevolent Authorities have insisted that as many objects as humanly possible should adopt an orange hue or related shades of rust, shrimp, mango, ochre, pumpkin, terra-cotta, mustard, mimosa, paw-paw, auricular wax or marmalade; and it is not surprising that this directive (inspired by a sloughed citrus rind) should also dictate the colour of the national sweetmeat, or *jaffa*, as well as the accoutrements and appurtenances of the Australian-based telecommunications system.

The NEW 1977-78
YELLOW PAGES
COMBINED BUYING GUIDE &
COMMERCIAL DIRECTORY

Welcome to the World's Biggest ORANGE

THE "BIG ORANGE"

16-METRE HIGH,

THE LARGEST FIBREGLASS SPHERE IN THE SOUTHERN HEMISPHERE

On the 3rd storey, a scenic lookout with commanding views of adjoining orchards, the river and scrubland

- "BIG ORANGE" TEA TOWELS, TEE-SHIRTS AND TEASPOONS
- RIVERLAND GIFT PACKS, CONTAINING A VARIETY OF LOCAL PRODUCE
- RIVERLAND SOUVENIRS
- RIVERLAND JAMS AND HONEY
- FRESH AND DRIED FRUIT

On the 2nd storey, there's a 360 panorama oil painting of the Riverland by well-known local artist,

95
95
95

ON STAGE
jaffas

TELEPHONE

Kangourou avec opale au Fabergé (*above*)
Solid gold gladiolus cluster (*left*)
As this book goes to press, the Authorities have not yet made it compulsory for citizens to wear jewellery which incorporates some acceptable and recognizable national *motif*. However, most top town and bushland *bijoutiers* are well stocked for such a move since they have always fashioned their exquisite pieces in forms richly suggestive of their unique *milieu*.

The traditional 'Toby' jug is here unequivocally translated into local idiom. Thinking Australians would think twice before quenching their thirst from any other vessel.

Fine marquetry Melbourne wall plaque with enamel kookaburras and poker-work inscription, and desk-top war memorial in burnished brass and polished nullabor elm with inset photograph vignettes. Querulous inhabitants of the island of Tasmania are rarely convinced that decorative and commemorative objects such as these pictured were fashioned before the discovery of their strange southern domain. Art historians and carbon-daters are giving increasing credence to the theory, however, that in fashioning unique *objets* such as I have illustrated the anonymous master craftsman has found the omission of the Tasmanian insular appendage expedient to the execution of his artistic and symbolic intentions.

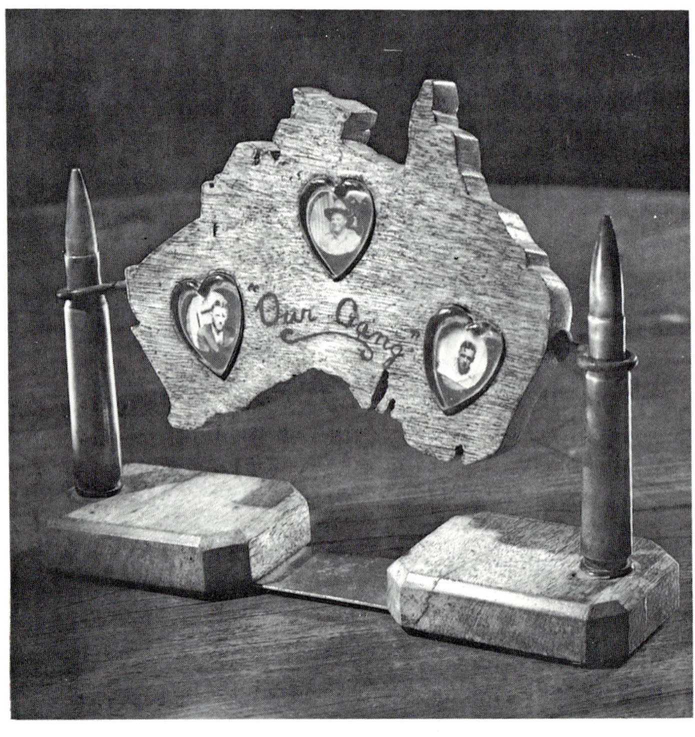

Although Australia's Federal and State Administrations seek to implement their long-term total demolition programme — as a 'final solution' to Australia's historic buildings problem — exceptions are sometimes made, and a few reprieved structures are sequestered and quietly deracinated in the small hours. The Sovereign Hill Conservation Camp outside Melbourne, in which classified erections are re-constituted where they cannot contaminate a modern and progressive ecosphere, is one of the few such camps in Australia open for supervised public inspection. The official photograph here reproduced should disprove subversive allegations claiming maltreatment of Australia's architectural heritage on the part of the Authorities.

Photograph: Michael Wennerich, Royal Melbourne Institute of Technology

'Old Sydney Town'. Re-sited buildings of historic importance immaculately maintained at a special location outside modern Sydney.

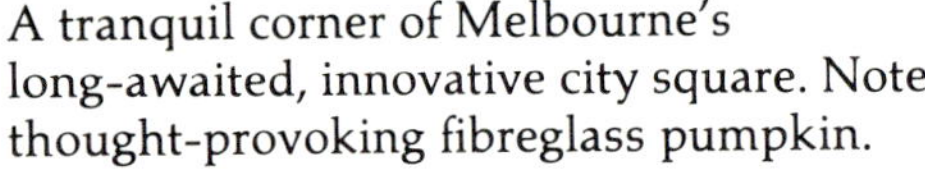

A tranquil corner of Melbourne's long-awaited, innovative city square. Note thought-provoking fibreglass pumpkin.

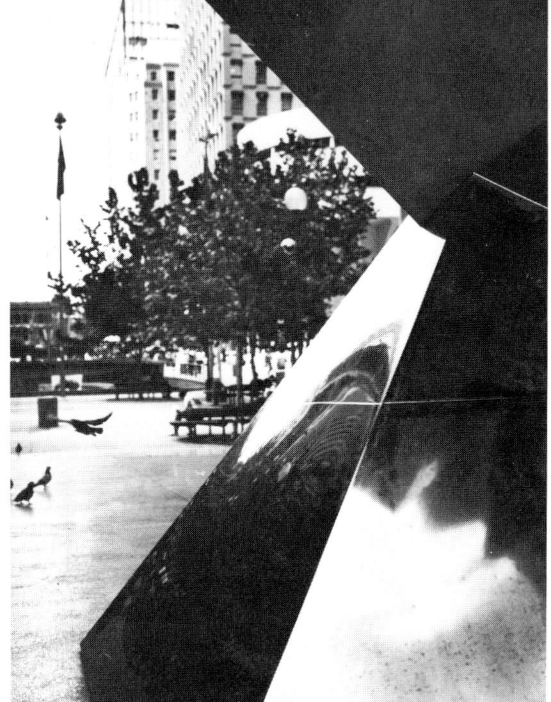

A tranquil corner of Sydney's imaginatively refurbished Martin Place precinct and leisure complex.

Photograph: Neville Coleman

The 'gummy' shark or *Carcharhinus galapagensis*. The popularity of this huge Australian fish may well be attributable to its absence of teeth.

Photographs : Rennie Ellis, Scoopix

Austral Mascots

Although the Kookaburra or 'laughing jackass' is one of our best loved birds, the sulphur-crested cockatoo keenly rivals it in popularity. Its psittacine virtues of intelligence and volubility are coincidentally Australian virtues. Australoids are rarely seen in city streets without an avian companion, like this senior citizen with her sagacious feathered 'familiar'.

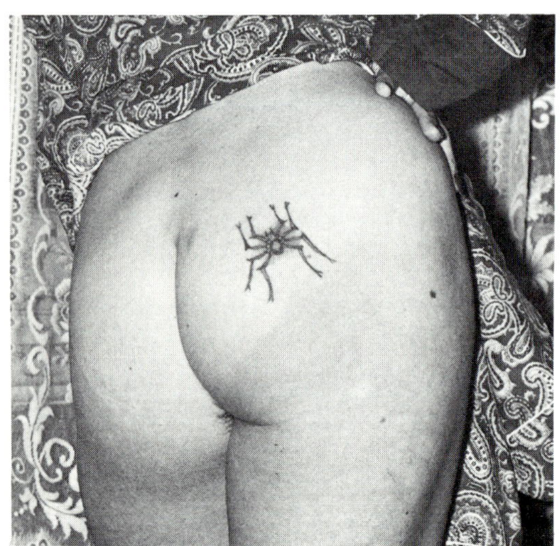

Most Australians are incorrigible arachniphiles, and like this young Sydney-based actress and feminist, they delight in embossing their cutaneous envelopes with the likeness of a favourite octopod.

You could win $1,000 or even $100,000 in 'The Age'-ANZ Landmark Contest

If you can think of a striking landmark — to be sited on 32 hectares of City property — you could win $1000 (or even $100,000) in "The Age" — ANZ Landmark Contest. In association with the ANZ bank, "The Age" is offering a first prize of $1,000, a second prize of $500 and ten consolation prizes of $100 each for the best ideas or designs submitted by "Age" readers. The two best entries received will then be improved up to professional standards and entered in the world-wide $100,000 Melbourne Landmark Competition.

The winning idea will be something striking — not necessarily a monument — which will focus world attention on Melbourne. Let your imagination run riot. Remember, all you have to do is come up with a great landmark IDEA for the space above the 32-hectare Jolimont railway yards between Princes Bridge, the Yarra, Flinders Street and Jolimont Road.

All we want is a GREAT IDEA, you may also submit a design or sketch but it is not necessary. The winning idea might even be expressed in just a few words. Hurry, because all entries must be received by this Saturday, June 30.

Send your entry to:

'The Age"-ANZ Landmark Contest, GPO Box 2070S, MELBOURNE, 3001

The judges decision will be final. No correspondence will be entered into. In the event of two similar ideas or designs being received, only the first one opened will be accepted. Employees of David Syme & Co. Ltd., publisher of "The Age" and their families are not permitted to enter the contest.

Hope for the future.

Acknowledgements

Colin Munro Esq.
Peter Thomson Photography
David Liddle Photography
Nigel Butterley Esq.
Susan Haynes
Sallyanne Moss
John Belot
Diane Millstead

The following details apply to paintings reproduced in this book:

Page 12, top:
Sydney Long, 1871–1955
The Music Lesson, 1904
Oil on canvas
28¼″ x 20¼″
Art Gallery of New South Wales

Page 12, below:
Russell Drysdale, b.1912
Sunday Evening. 1940
Oil on canvas
29¾″ x 23½″
Art Gallery of New South Wales

Page 13, top:
John Brack, b.1920–
Barry Humphries in the character of Mrs. Everage. 1969
Oil on canvas
37 1/5″ x 50½″
Art Gallery of New South Wales

Page 13, left:
William Dobell 1899–1970
Dame Mary Gilmore, 1957
Oil on masonite
35½″ x 29″
Art Gallery of New South Wales
Gift of Dame Mary Gilmore, 1960

Page 13, right:
Albert Tucker
Intruder 1967/8
Acrylic
48″ x 36″
Collection: the artist